UNBELIEVABLE STORIES OF SIMONE BILES

THIS BOOK BELONGS TO:

© 2021, Kids Castle Press. All rights reserved. No part of this publication may be reproduced, stored, distributed, or transmitted, in any form or by means, including photocopying, recording, or other electronic or mechanical methods, without prior written permission of the publisher, except in the case of brief quotations embodied in critical reviews and certain other noncommercial uses permitted by copyright law.

UNBELIEVABLE STORIES OF

SIMONE BILES

INTRODUCTION

Simone Biles is an American gymnast who is famous worldwide. You might have seen videos of her amazing gymnastic routines or even watched her on television. Simone has competed in both the Olympics and the World Championships.

She performs on the vault, balance beam, floor exercise, and parallel bars. Simone is short and powerful, and also has a friendly smile. Her happiness and smiles are well deserved, and she has won many medals. In fact, Simone has won more gold medals than any other gymnast in history.

Simone inspires us with her ability to overcome unbelievable challenges to achieve amazing things.

Chapter 1:

Early Challenges

Simone was born March 17, 1997, in Columbus, Ohio. She has one older brother, named Tevin, and one older sister, named Ashley. Her younger sister, Adria, is only 2 years younger than her. When she was a child, Simone thought, "We are two peas in a pod. Adria and I look so much alike, people are sure that we are twins." Not only do they look alike, but they both compete in gymnastics.

Simone began taking gymnastics lessons when she was 6. Adria looked up to her older sister so much that she wanted to follow in her footsteps. Simone was so good at gymnastics that her teachers were delighted. They told her to keep taking lessons and practicing because she would be a star someday.

When Simone was very young, her mother was ill and struggled with taking care of her and her brother and sisters. That's why, Simone and her siblings were put into foster care, which is where another family takes care of children who need some help. Foster care families are only for a short period of time.

Simone and her siblings would go home for a while with their mother and then had to go back into foster care. Sometimes children in foster care get separated from their brothers and sisters, luckily that didn't happen often with Simone, but it was still hard to be taken care of by other families. She missed feeling safe and having her family live together.

After a few years of not having a permanent home, a miracle happened. When Simone was 6 and Adria was 4, her grandparents offered to adopt the two younger girls. They wanted to give the sisters a permanent home, so they asked them if they wanted to be adopted. Being adopted meant leaving behind their older brother and sister. It would also mean that they would have to leave Ohio and move to Texas, which is across the country!

Simone said, "I have always wanted to have a family that is together, so the answer is yes." Adria agreed, too, and both girls were excited that they no longer had to worry about living in different homes.

Since she was adopted at the age of 6, Simone has called her grandparents Mom and Dad. Simone's family are strong supports and until the COVID pandemic set restrictions on attending gymnastic competitions, her family had attended every single one! Simone now has an amazing family that supports and loves her very much.

Chapter 2:

Learning to Love Herself

At school, Simone seemed to always be the shortest person in class. She was also shorter than her friends, who were the same age. Simone used to wonder if she would ever grow enough and catch up with them. Sometimes she felt self-conscious about being short. Especially when the other kids would call her "shrimp" or "shorty."

"I wish I wasn't so short," she complained to her coach. Her coach smiled and told her not to worry so much. She told her, "Gymnasts who are short have more power. Because you are short, you are ahead of the taller gymnasts." Simone smiled and practiced shifting her thinking to remind herself that being short is a good thing.

As Simone continued to pursue her love of gymnastics, she became more and more muscular. Gymnasts, like most athletes, exercise their muscles a lot and, as a result, often have strong muscles that everyone can see. When Simone was still in school, her classmates would tease her about being muscular.

At first she tried to hide her muscles, but then Simone changed her mind. She said, "I wouldn't be able to achieve the things I did without my body." This is a great example of how Simone practiced gratitude for her strength and muscles. It takes a lot of courage for someone to ignore people making fun of your body. Making the choice to ignore the hurtful remarks, Simone set her focus on getting better at gymnastics.

Being teased and bothered by others didn't stop at school. When practicing gymnastics, sometimes the other gymnasts would be mean or leave her out of activities that they did together. Even today that Simone has grown up and became an adult, the bullying has not stopped.

Once at a competition, Simone was made fun of because her hair had a different texture than some of her teammates. Unfortunately, many people of color continue to experience people saying harmful and hurtful things to them every day, just like Simone. Despite the mean and disrespectful behavior, Simone continues to shine bright in the face of adversity and be an inspiration. She has said, "I just have to keep going for those little ones looking up to me."

Chapter 3:

Simone Is Unique

When Simone was younger, she noticed that she acted a little differently than some other children her age. During a Science lesson, Simone was picturing herself twirling and spinning on the gymnasium floor. "Stop, she would tell herself, you are at school now, not at practice."

A few minutes later, she heard her teacher ask, "Simone, what is the force that brings you back to the ground when you jump?" Simone squirmed in her seat and said, "I don't know." Of course, Simone did know about gravity. She used that force every day while training in gymnastics.

Another time, Simone's family was watching a movie together. Simone was having a blast somersaulting off the couch over and over. Then, she looked over at Adria to see if she was also having a great time. Adria was having a great time, but she was sitting still.

Eventually, Simone went to the doctor with her parents. The doctor did some tests on her, then told Simone that she had ADHD. That stands for Attention-Deficit Hyperactivity Disorder.

Simone was a little scared. "Will I be very sick?" she asked. "You are not sick at all," said her doctor. "There are many people, adults and children who also have ADHD. It is just a part of you that makes you unique," her parents told her.

Simone soon learned that she not only had to train her body, she also had to train her mind to be able to focus more. She began to take medicine and made a plan to help her manage her ADHD. Simone decided that just because she had ADHD, that didn't mean she wasn't smart.

When Simone was competing at the 2016 Olympics, many people discovered that she had ADHD. Some people thought that meant that she shouldn't compete. A reporter asked her if she was embarrassed that the world knew.

“Of course not,” Simone answered. “I am unique and ADHD is just a part of me. A part that I love and am not embarrassed by.”

Her answer gave many people around the world courage to also love themselves. She showed them how to love themselves for the things that made them unique. All the years that Simone spent training in gymnastics made her a strong athlete. All the years that she also spent training her mind made her a strong person.

Chapter 4:
First World Championship

Gymnasts don't just compete in the Olympics. There are many competitions. Another very important gymnastics competition is the World Championships. In 2014, Simone traveled with her teammates to China to compete in the World Championships.

Simone was very excited, but also very nervous. Earlier that year, she had a shoulder injury and had to sit out of two other important competitions. When Simone entered the grand arena and saw all of the cameras, her heart began to race.

"Take a deep breath," she told herself. "Close your eyes, and count to 10." Simone did just that and instantly felt much better. She opened her eyes, squeezed the hand of her teammate and said, "Let's do this." She was ready to perform her best during her routine and cheer her teammates on during theirs.

Simone was wearing a sparkly pink leotard, her team's chosen uniform, and was prepared to give it her best. She performed very well on the thin balance beam, jumping and dismounting beautifully. Simone also flipped and spun her way through a great floor exercise routine, her favorite.

Then, it was time for her to tackle the uneven bars. Even though Simone had practiced her routine over and over, this event has always been a challenge for her. As all eyes and cameras were on her, she swung over the high bar and accidentally put her foot on it. The crowd gasped and Simone was disappointed.

"I have to do my best the rest of the routine," she told herself. "Keep going." Simone finished the routine and recovered from her error with grace. Simone was awarded the gold medal for best all-around athlete in the World Championships.

When a gymnast earns a medal, there is a ceremony where they stand on a podium to receive it. The Gold Medal gymnast stands in the middle of the podium, with Silver to their left and Bronze on their right. Each is given a bouquet of beautiful flowers.

That year, Simone's teammate and friend, Kyla Ross, won the Bronze, so she was standing to Simone's right.

Simone and Kyla were both presented with their medals and flowers. But Kyla noticed something was not quite right with the bouquet. The flowers were so fresh that they attracted bees!

Kyla quickly whispered to Simone and warned her about the bee. Simone did what any other 16-year-old would do. She giggled and jumped off the podium to escape the little pest. This moment was caught on camera and viewed by many, who appreciated seeing a more silly side of Simone.

Chapter 5:

Not Just a Gymnast!

Simone is considered one of the greatest gymnasts ever. Each week, she spends on average 32 hours at the gym practicing her routines. Sometimes, when she is done practicing, Simone will stay at the gym, inventing new moves.

Even though Simone is considered one of the greatest gymnasts ever, there is so much more to her than practicing routines. Unfortunately being a gymnast isn't a life long career because it becomes harder and harder to do routines the older our bodies grow. Knowing this, Simone has been thoughtful not just focusing her life only on gymnastics.

Simone loves dogs! She grew up with 4 German Shepards that she loves to play with in her free time. "They are kind of like my other siblings," she insists. Simone also has two dogs of her own! They are French Bulldogs, Lilo and Rambo, they bring laughter and joy to her life. Simone has shared how they can make her laugh and help her feel supported and cared for as she trains for her routines.

Simone's favorite food is pizza, especially if it is topped with pepperoni. She loves to gather her friends and family and catch up over a slice.

Simone is passionate about make up! "I really like my eyes to stand out during competition," she says. She spends hours coordinating her eye shadow to her uniforms. "I want them to be just as sparkly and noticeable as my leotards."

Simone also enjoys reading fashion magazines. When she isn't in her beautiful sparkly leotards, she is wearing the current fashion trends! Simone has even done modeling. She got to be on the cover of the famous fashion magazine, Vogue. This is just another way that Simone inspires others, despite people trying to make her believe she isn't beautiful. Simone has been willing to share her incredible beauty with the world through her modeling, gymnastics, and her kind heart.

Chapter 6:

Breaking Through Barriers

Simone likes to see how far she can push her skills, it is not enough for her to just perfect a move. With her coaches she tries to add another flip or turn to keep pushing the boundaries of gymnastic moves. When Simone is able to successfully add something of her own to a gymnastic move, it creates a new move and it gets to be named after Simone. Simone continues to add to the legacy of gymnastics, she has one move on her floor routine named The Biles.

To perform it, Simone has to flip twice in the air and make her body straight. Then, she adds a half twist at the very end. This half twist means that she cannot see where she is about to land.

One of Simone's amazing skills in gymnastics is her close relationship with her body while it is moving in the air. This enables her to do moves that other gymnasts will not do for fear of injury.

Sometimes, Simone invents a move that is so dangerous that the judges make it worth less points. They do this because Simone is the only gymnast who can perform it. The judges are worried that others will try it and injure themselves.

"I don't think that is fair, but I am going to do it anyway," said Simone.

This move is known as The Biles on the Balance Beam. Simone was getting ready to perform it at the 2019 World Championships. She had on a purple leotard with a matching bow and a determined look on her face. She was on the beam, ready to dismount so she could do two flips in the air while also doing two twists. The crowd held their breath, afraid that Simone would fall or hurt herself. Simone stuck her landing with a big grin on her face.

Simone was competing in the GK US Classic Games of 2021. There, she was determined to perform a vault skill called the Yurchenko Double Pike. This move was so difficult, no other female gymnast had performed it in competition before.

Simone had practiced and perfected it for a long time. She wanted to show the world how strong women can be.

"I am going to let my gymnastics speak for me," she said.

Simone first performed a round-off onto the springboard. She then turned into a back handspring onto the vault. Next, she did a piked double backflip and nailed the landing.

Simone showed strength and determination. She has become much more than just a gymnast, she is a legend!

Chapter 7:

Going to the Olympics!

Simone competed in competitions all around the world, but her dream was to compete in the Olympics. In the Summer of 2016, her time finally came. She traveled to Rio de Janeiro, Brazil to compete in the Olympics.

Just because she was on the American team did not mean that she could automatically compete. First, Simone had to show the judges just how talented she was.

On her first day, she was nervous again. She kept thinking about her mistake at the World Championships. She was also worried that she could injure herself and be disqualified.

"Think about all the other girls who are looking up to you," she thought. She decided to not be afraid of achieving her dream and qualified. Simone and her teammates called themselves "The Final Five."

Simone was set to compete in 4 gymnastic events at the Olympics: floor exercise, balance beam, uneven bars and vault.

Before she competed in the vault, she was feeling very nervous. The most important part of the vault is the landing. If she makes a misstep or move even a little bit, the judges will notice and take points off of her score.

Simone told herself not to worry. "On the vault, you have two tries but make both of them count." Simone ran toward the vault with determination and flipped through the air like she was flying.

Simone was haunted by her error on the Uneven Bars during the World Championships. “I wanted to give up after my mistake,” she told herself. “I didn’t give up for one second, instead I finished the routine.”

For the first few days Simone was scoring high. But when she got to her performance on the individual balance beam, things changed. Simone was doing a front tuck and she didn’t rotate all the way. To catch herself from falling, she put her hand on the balance beam for a second. Simone was disappointed but she finished the routine.

Even though things didn’t go the way Simone had hoped they would, she won a bronze medal (3rd place) for her work on the balance beam. Along with her bronze medal, Simone went on to earn 4 gold medals while at the 2016 Olympics!

Chapter 8:

Nothing Stops Simone

During the 2018 World Championships, Simone was not feeling well. She had something called kidney stones! Kidney stones produce unexpected pain in the kidneys, which is a part of our body that helps us get rid of waste from the body. Sometimes someone with kidney stones can spend a lot of time in bed, taking days to recover.

Simone spent the night before her event in the emergency room, but she knew her team was counting on her to help get the gold medal! She said, "The kidney stones can wait, I'm doing it for my team."

She got up the next morning and went to the competition.

Some people thought that meant that her kidney stones were gone. They weren't. Simone decided that she did not have time to get them taken out before competition.

That means that Simone was still feeling a great deal of pain.

When she was asked how she could perform while in pain, Simone just smiled. "I still feel a little pain when I am walking or stretching," she said. She said she was simply too excited to quit.

Her body was producing a lot of adrenaline. Adrenaline is the human response to potentially dangerous situations. It makes people want to either fight harder or run away. Simone chose to fight harder for herself and her team.

Simone's decision to still compete showed strength and determination. Simone performed another vault move that was named after her. It is called the Biles II.

She performed a beautiful and powerful balance beam routine. She earned the most points in this routine for her team. She also earned the most points for her team in the vault and her floor exercise.

Her team ended up with the largest point victory in history. Simone did not stop there. She went on the next day to win a gold medal in the floor exercise and a bronze medal on the balance beam. Simone left the competition in Doha feeling like a champion inside and out.

Chapter 9:

Everyone Needs Role Models

Simone Biles is a hero, an icon, and an inspiration to many people around the world. She, like many other athletes, look to the best in their sport to learn from and to be inspired. Simone's gymnast icon is Alicia Sacramone.

"I want to be just like her," Simone said. "If I could be her mini-me, I would."

Alicia Sacramone is also an American gymnast. She specialized in the floor exercise, which is also a favorite of Simone's. Alicia has also won medals in the vault and balance beam. Alicia held the world record for the woman with the most World Championship Medals, with 10. One year later, Simone buzzed past her by earning 11 medals and the new World Record.

Early in her career, Simone wanted to follow the same path as Alicia. Alicia was known for the floor exercise, balance beam, and vault. She famously did not like to compete on the bars because she did not think she was good enough.

Simone also thought that she was weak in the bar events. It did not bother her though, because her idol did not need them in order to do well. Simone thought, "I am going to be exactly like her and be a specialist on three events."

There was one person who did not agree with that plan, Simone's coach, Aimee Boorman. She did not want Simone to settle for three events, when she could be good at four.

Simone took her coach's advice and worked even harder on the bars. Simone now thinks that she is "wired like a robot" because her bar skills are so good.

Simone also looks up to Gabby Douglas. Gabby was the first African-American gymnast to win in the All-Around Championship in 2012.

Simone remembers watching Gabby compete on television in London at the 2012 Olympics. She was encouraged and inspired by seeing Gabby's success as an African American woman winner of an Olympic gold medal.

"All of the sudden, everybody wanted to take gymnastics," Simone said. Simone set herself a goal to compete in the next Olympic Games.

Luckily, Simone and Gabby got to be teammates in the 2016 Olympics. They worked together with 3 other teammates to win the team the gold medal in artistic gymnastics.

Chapter 10:

Simone Changes the World, Again!

Simone went to the 2020 Tokyo Olympics with the sense that all eyes were on her. Many people thought that she was bound to beat previous records and win a lot of gold medals for the United States.

These Olympic Games were different than previous years, the games had pushed back a whole year due to COVID-19. The global pandemic had been just as stressful for Simone as it had been for people all over the world. The arena, where Simone performed her events, was different too. No one could watch the athletes, it was only the athletes, the people with the cameras and a few people who had to be there to help.

"I feel like I have the weight of the world on my shoulders," Simone confessed. In the past, Simone had pushed through challenges, and she felt like she had to do that again.

Simone's first even was the vault. When Simone was in the air, she only completed 1.5 twists instead of the 2.5 she was had planned. She nearly fell on the landing but luckily landed safely.

Simone knows her body and has a lot of experience competing. She knows that without focus, she could be risking her life. Simone recognized that her mind and her body were not in sync and, for her own safety, she made the difficult decision to withdraw from the team competition.

By doing this, Simone accidentally became famous for taking care of her mental health, or the health of her mind. She reminded the fans watching at home, that athletes are not just performers, that they are also people.

USA

Many people thought that Simone had betrayed her team and country by stepping back to take care of herself, even knowing that she did it to keep herself safe. After a few days of rest, Simone decided to come back to the Olympics and try again; her determination to keep competing shining through.

Simone decided to compete on the balance beam. Even though her routine didn't go as she had practiced, it was still amazing! She won the bronze medal, just as she had in the 2016 Olympics.

Simone said,"This medal means more to me than all the ones before, even the golds." Simone continues to show that she is one of the world's greatest athletes through her determination and perseverance.

THE END

Made in the USA
Columbia, SC
15 February 2024